Love in the Environs of Voronezh

AND OTHER POEMS

by Alan Sillitoe

1969

Doubleday & Company, Inc. GARDEN CITY, NEW YORK

Library of Congress Catalog Card Number 68–9189
Copyright © 1968 by Alan Sillitoe
Printed in the United States of America
First Edition in the United States of America

CONTENTS

*Love
in the Environs
of Voronezh*

AND OTHER POEMS

Burned out, burned out.
Water of rivers hold me
On a course towards sea.
Burned out was like a tree
Cut down and hollowed
Seasoned by skilful
Fire into a boat:
Burned out through love
Or the heart's wilful spending
I'm sure it will float
And kindle a new blaze
To burn itself right out again
On some strange shore—
Unless pyromaniac emotions
Catch me in midstream
And the sun turns black.

Man and wife
Or sister and brother
Or mistress and lover—
They were made for each other
He for him and she for her
As if out of one mother.
They loved one another.

Made for each other
 He got him and she got her
Got each other
Without any bother
Married one autumn
Bedded completely
Made for each other.

No need to wait and see
Whether she will smother him
Or he will smother her.
They were made for each other;
And that's all that matters.

Gun, gas, greatest height,
Cataclysm in a motorcar—
Think of it without thought
But never do it.

Ice cannot melt
Unless by selfpity or emotion.
Stones that weigh so hard
In heart and body

Are like those that sink ships
To form a harbour—
Against which clean ocean crashes
Till such ballast festers in victory—

And holds back the earth,
And keeps out the sea
And sends ships safely
On uncharted journeys.

They share this window:
Rain smokes down between trees
And soil drinks.

Hands burn bushes that cannot be reached
Scorch rain
Turn to smoke that drifts around leaves.
The sky eases his skull.

Air moves, disguised as rain, between
Trees that caught her glance
That passed between them in this wooden house
These bones of wax
That widening ink-split of the sky
Fast running out—

They call it love
A vicious loneliness
An only child of forest and retreat
Which makes her laugh (and him)
Love, and his consort, love
When her glowing eyes turn.

Every dream is held back by a paper wall
With the sea behind it
A nightmare heart-thin wafer
Keeping off the ocean's blinding spite
And always about to split
Under razor-treading feet
That walk along the top of it—
And on the other side an endless drop.

There is no tide
In the grey surface kicking at the rim.
At a point impossible to find
Invisible force will press
And burst the boundary of sky:
All lovers and bad dreamers
Will fall first,
If that wall should ever break,
Torn by an eagle's razoring beak.

He fell in love like an arrow flying
Arrived and fought until trophied
And atrophied, entered as if she
Were a corpse concealing golden booty
He'd never dreamed of reaching.
What else could a moving dead man do
Among such diamonds and glitter?

Each woman loved him for his boldness
Baked him in lust until almost living
Gave him hair and skin and tiger-eyes
While he beat loud on the drum of his emptiness
And called it the only sort of love
The love that sacrifices everything for love—
Which warned no one off:
Loved them inhumanly till they became
Passionless, thinlipped and grey
Stared at the arid landscape
Into which he retreated, smiling, smiling.

To keep them comfortably in thrall
They build a fire in the hall
And burn their beautiful house to ash.
A ruin is better than no love at all—

Black and solitary timbers crash
The cats surround it at full moon.
Did they abandon it too soon
Full of happiness to see it fall?

Let it fall, in sight of all
It kept them long enough in thrall
As cupboards burn and timbers fall.

They're still inside, with all doors locked
No windows through which one can crawl:
Only the trapped and burning see it fall.

It kept them miserably in thrall.
A ruin is better than no love at all.
They smile with happiness to see it fall.

Life must go on, he said,
Sliding the knife deeper.
Lips are sealed by my heart,
And blood congeals
To keep all poisons in.

Romeo was forty years old today
And Juliet took yet another lover.
He picked an artichoke to bits
Eating none of it
Not even knowing if he loved her:
I do, I don't, I do, I don't.

At the end of a long walk in the city
He sat on a wasteground where some factory
Would fungus up to pull him in—
After he'd bled to death
Out of a half-born will.

Sword fixing him to air of fire:
No post will hold him up.
Electrified in life's pintable game
Pain pushes him to the next
Light or flag or cinderpost.
No score, no score, pulled
Clear by shock and memory
From doors which cannot open
To another totem pole
Or flight of steps. Will
He drop there? Reach one more?
Does not remember, when
A flag falls and the final lights go out
Which trap took him in
Nor what lit up its dark inside.

Bullet, bomb
Arm off, head gone
Hole is, limb black
Where sun shone.

Shutter works, puppet walks
Sky winks energy and guile,
Howitzer at chimneystack
Scorches out your smile.

One life, earth turning
Tuning up its brilliant wax,
Birth is burning out
An axe to razor off the leaves:

Dolls and effigies below
Rot in soil where flowers grow.

War on cancer, its racist face
A whitewinged flamethrower spreading to
Swampblood or innocent veins,
A wall-moat hemming victims in:

Quicksilver enemies spread and cling
Till the inhabitants are rats in a single box.
That do not break but only suffer
By the blinkered useless heart numbed
At never meeting the true intelligence
And freedom in them,
Their right that never could be had
Till the body sensed they had grown used
To such futility, then took command
To be ensured of victory.

Conquer the bullet tearing through. The final
Hand grenade turns blue when it explodes.
The road diverges in the wood, illness one way
Death another. Day loves its junctions, night
Its forks, dusk eludes a circle and false dawn
Its cross. There is no loss when the body walks
Through swamp and forest, towards burning desert
From which there is no turning.

As the moon grew
Its eyes could not wane
Lost their sight in gazing
To blue mist and fen-haze
And holland fire-lace of dusk.

Hopeful and lonely, lunar growth
Warmed its fish-shaped womb
Both skins stretching bigger
At searching for each other.

Moonblind: magic blinkers
Blind to the lunarstone's
Heavy lumping as it walked—
Head elongated, nostrils flowering
Eyes a double moon to all beholders.

It held the moon
That wanted to get right out
That came to lock a horse inside the moon
And have it riding roughshod through,
Waxing limitless
And perishing in radiant beams.

1

Those who gamble
And their opposites, lovers
And their destroyers, soldiers
Come in turn and claim
With lack of fine intelligence
(To put it bluntly, as a one-time
Victim of all three should)
That they join their memories
With this present minute of today:

It is a trick, he knows, betting on whether
She will or won't, as a lover will,
And preparing his retreat, as a soldier should.

He had lost his courage
But not all desire:
The ice in his stomach
Could put out no fire:

He smiled at the midnight prostitute moon
And her customer stars,
Looked through the trees of the forest
While fire clawed into the gut of loverheart
The laughs of heaven and honey
He found no sweeter than this great
Flame-grin of the world's new-risen whore.
Good riddance, and the lovers are
Dead ash in someone's craw:
There are always more to follow
Into the cannonmouth of love
And the cunt of war, till flames
Catch up with both and end it all,
The last ash and even smoke of it.
He had lost her, and for good
But fell in love with another
And began the battlefodder
Again towards lightning horizons
And midnight-midday frostbitten forest fires
Burning into the dust and honeymilk
And eating even the iron through.

To burn out love is to burn a star from the sky
No eye can do it and no touch can reach that far
But madness feels the fire increase
Scorching the heart but not the star that burns

Star that beats in me like a fish
My heart meets whether dark or light
In the inland waters of the star.
Such love can never be put out
If I've no power or wish to break
My brain and fist against that star.

Orange-lit night blocked into London—
And a fire-engine races through
A freak snowstorm
With all bells hurting the air.
Will it skid into oblivion
At the next shop corner
And leave only the snow of heaven
To put all fires out?
The heart of the night is white
But around the edges it glows red:

A rocket trail through traffic
Turns to the heart's deepest blaze,
An insane leavening of eardrums
As snow drifts over all useless passion
Spreading roughshod from the moon.

A hearse at morning's four o'clock
Draws its purple hood through Knightsbridge—
Hooves, feathers, wheels and varnished plywood
Vanishing in whitest snow.

A broad and solid oak exploded
Split by mystery and shock
Broken like bread
Like a flower shaken.
Acorn guts dropped out
A dead gorilla unlocked from breeding trees,
Acorns with death in their baby eyes.

A hang-armed scarecrow in the wind
What hit it? got into it? struck so quietly
Between dawn and daylight?
With a dying grin and wooden wink
A lost interior cell relinquished its own ghost:
In full spleen and abundant acorn
A horn of lightning gored it to the quick.

Trees move on Fenland
Uprooting men and houses on a march
To reach their enemy the sea.
Silent at the smell of watersalt
Treelines advance. The sea lies low
Snake-noise riding on unruffled surf
While all trees wither and retreat.

Out of farmrange or cottage eyes trees make war
Green heads close as if to kiss
Roots to rip at quickening wood of tree-hearts
And tree-lungs, sap-running wood-flesh
Hurled at the moon, breaking oak
Like the dismemberment of ships
At the truce of dawn wind trumpeting.

Sedate, dispassionate and beautiful
They know about panic and life and patience
Grow by guile into night's
Companions and day's evil
Setting landmarks and boundaries
That continually fight the worms.

Trees love, love love, love death
Love a windscorched earth and copper sky
Love the burns of ice and fire
When lightning as a last hope is called in.
Boats on land they loathe the sea
And wait with all arms spread to catch the moon:
Pull back my skin and there is bark
Peel off my bark and there is skin
I am a tree whose roots destroy me.

Fiddletongue and spite
Hang fire as if he sleeps
Safe on his tipped-up world—
But lizard-shoulders hunch
At a fly on the slanted wall.

Belly smooth, and feet stuck firm
Hold a thousand volts of paralysing tongue
To rifle out and kill—
Guts and weapon in one stomach pit.

Death is quick when looked on,
Sweet as food when the lights of paradise
Blacken a brain that one day
Hoped to know them.

A sparking tongue ignites
A common wink of death
Between you and me,
And the lizard eating as it runs,
Unaware of being upside down.

THE KNIGHT IN PANTHER'S SKIN

from Shot'ha Rust'hveli.

I crossed the reedgrass and came to a hill
Where a lion and a panther walked together
As if deep in love, pacific lovers
That subdued my own upbeating fires.

Suddenly they closed in bitter struggle
Out of amorous grooming came a deadly
Quarrel, of lion pursuing panther
In a fight that terrified my soul.

Each clubbed the other with its paws
Not fearing death. But the panther
Lost hope like a woman, and the
Ungovernable lion bore him down.

I loathed that lion's viciousness:
"Why savage what you love and call it valour?"
Rushed with my uncovered sword and cleaved
Him from the travail of this world.

I let go my sword to hold the panther in my arms
And kiss it like the one who burns in me,
But with no quiet heart it roared and circled
Paws bloodsharp till I could bear no more—

Soothing was futile: with tightening hand
I thrust its life out on the ground.
So I had striven with my beloved,
Yet nothing could wrench the dark night from me.

Though life is not natural, neither
Will death take me. Between me and the world
Is a land I cannot cross. Is it strange
That I despair and weep?

You pander to a suicide: love him,
Her, all that's left
Sandwiches scuffed
On the kitchen floor
That comical black eye—
Inkdot into which
Life poured to kill itself
As if a fire burned there
And a gale flattened it.
Love cannot grow again
Or rub out death
In whoever stays behind.

You pander to a suicide
Sorry for him
Her, it; glad it was not me,
Love myself, won't eat sandwiches
Or ease that poor eye—
Love myself and am a pander
Saying he, she, it did no wrong
Could not entertain the world
Nor the world it.
And you, futile and pandering
Could never face nor pander to
Simple inexpedients of pure sorrow.

End of life and before death
A bird was flying
Feathers dipping towards oaken frost
Heard that shot
Burst the ink sky open
Stone colliding with sun

An echo stunned its wing
String hauled it down.
Gamekeeper or poacher—what could
It care? cut out of
Free flight to the sea.

Vise had tongue, veins, teeth
Dogs in panoply, firm pressure
Carry it to a sunspot fitting neat
The blacked-out circle of a gun.

A small man formed
One hour after spinning into light
Body-brain wrapped and only blue eyes
Open to noise of rook and cuckoo
To stalk a rabbit in the woods
Read a book, stay nothing less than
Blank before sudden turns
To evergreen or glint of water.

Hirsute and stern on bleak arrival
He lay down after a toiler's day,
Face inclined to say: All right,
You gave me life, but death also.

Forehead creased on future worry
When hacking obstacles;
Indenting map-hair on a moving palm
To say it doesn't matter, go to sleep.
Such lifeline struck a horoscope:
Luck-speedkid-devil with women
Which his years will balance
In give and take, or ruination—
Seeing all but never everything.

So goodnight sweet baby, sleep
Safe in the uplands of oblivion
Beyond the iced bite of the moon.
You are what you feel this minute
Free with innocence but lacking milk
Soon to become all that you do not feel—

Hoping to advance against
Only the normal hazarding inroads
That spin life down into havoc
Have power to dissect visions
Like the yoke and mucus of an egg:
And walk the uplands of oblivion
To build up certain freedoms from the moon.

MIXED UP MYSTIC THOUGHTS OF
A MIDWESTERN MISSILE MAN

Dear God, receive my elevated rocket
Bollock black and turbulent untombed at last
That scorches neither hair nor logic—
I'm praying with one buttonfinger free while you God
Drunken queer old autocratic bastard rave above it
Strapped in your art-nouveau chair to watch
The final boiling spew-cock of the world
On its uprush towards home and heaven.

Once as a boy you held my hand
(You more sacred than any toy machine or gun)
Which I remember
And could not forgive you letting go.
I walked complete that ancient summer
And even when I cried You still let go.
When winter comes I eat the snow.

This bomb is coming, God,
To fertilize your desert heaven:
Don't turn the other cheek
And send it spinning to a megadeath
But understand that Christ is risen
And ring a countdown on the bells
At your new son swelling up and out to get you
For that black crucifixion foistered once—
The foaming jackpot climbing high
To clean all cobwebs from the sky,
Obliterate your magic eye.

Evade the guide, and walk a tunnel of your own,
Eat toadstools and loganberries, lamp in hand,
The brain that did these paintings is a fullstop
At the end of each cavemouth,
A black dot pinned on a mountainwall
A black dot vast in smokestains
Pleurisy and liverfluke
Animals of bloodsmear and blackhead eyes.

You get lost in that black dot
Tread loganberry stumps
And toadstool scraps, till eyes
Open into sealight and space to live
A wilderness beyond never-set limits.

It deceives you:
That black empire of a dot
Is a tumour on the brain
A star extinguished as the sea pours in.
Turn back and run; leave it to drown—
Fresh air is better
Than that fish-roar of mist and violence.

He meditates on the empty quarter:
Mosque of sand dissolving through eggtimer's
Neck. Looks on camel-loads
Starting for Oman or Muscat
By invisible mercator's thread,
That burns the hoof and shrivels up
All humps of water. Empty quarter lures,
He travels with his own heaped caravan
On earth-tracks marked as lines
Of an unstable hand, golden sandgrit
Lifting up grey land near vulcan-
Trees and foul magnesium wells that asps
And camels drink from.
He throws off bells, beads, silk, guns,
Knives and slippers, scattering all
No longer needed or outlived—camel meat
For guides and scavengers, everything
To his own dishrags and flesh.
Naked, demented, abandoned, he hugs
One tree rooted in the widest waste:
Catches dew that forms at dawn
And dates dropping through rottenness,
Tastes its shade, a lone tree
No one can chop or whip him from,
Till one day ravelled in his own white flame
He turns from the empty quarter—
And trudges back to bore and terrify the world.

Can't get him out.
Sits in the fireplace, right inside
Too far in, curled-up tight
Where olive logs sent red and runting flames
Feeling the chimney spout.

Cold and safe, legs drawn up,
Wan smile, squats in his fireplace,
Irons cold, hair neat, right in,
Away and safe from all of us—
Unless someone has a crowbar
And no heart to prise him whimpering free—
Smiling wanly because no one has.

If and when, he'd be a normal
Dead man on the street, and he smiles
At this mirror that no one can smash,
Moonless smile of victory
Insane and constant as the sun
That cleanses better than the fire
Or this prison that it once burned in.

The river has burst its banks
Churches and cathedrals slide away—
Blue cloud pulling at each spire
Hillocks shoving from behind . . .

Those several channels now are one wide lake
That wide and leisurely meandering is gone
You cannot shout from one side to the other—
You try to swim and get dragged out to sea.

There was no rain to swell the river
Nor any fissure shot it from below
But that slow river is now fledged and roaring
Collapsing all its banks and spreading wide.

The spire and nave and transept crumble in
The branches of a tree catch on it to be saved:
Children laugh and crayon in another sun
To join the other six and dry this river up

This forceput monster eating at the land
Where tree and spire sink back to the fishes:
Every shore is melting fast
From that unholy water pulling villages and cities in.

Parsley hair
Radish eyes
Lettuce ears
Apple nose
And potato lips—

Turnip body
Cabbage breasts
Celery arms
And carrot legs—

She is the goddess of the earth:
I found her under the willow tree.

THOSE STUPID LITTLE TRUMPETS OF THE LORD

Those stupid little trumpets of the Lord
That occasionally echo in the hills
Do not make me angry or feel bored
Enough to close the window at their trills.

I don't know where they come from, or much care
Sit listening at my desk and stare
Out the hills as if to see their noise.
Looking back into myself destroys

Their threat, and I wonder what in me can cause
These futile sounds to play,
If all my shame and nullity will force
Them to be silent. But when the present day

Breaks back and the trumpets of the Lord still sound
I go out and walk towards the rising ground
And stand in perfect silence, and know
That I could only hear them far below.

A house blocks out the sky
Keeps you clear of Heaven's flash
Is a hollow cork in the earth
Skin beyond skin
A shelter to adorn or pull you into ruin.

A house is the safest form of love
That turns a lavish white at Candlemas
Terrifies all simple villagers
And vanishes an hour before dawn.

A place where torment flourishes
A grin of loonybins locked bright within
Goes rotten at its moon beams
When some anguished family
In a last united gesture
Batters its way out.

A wild cat savaged my hand
Bit deep into the flesh and poisoned it.
What reason had I to reach out and touch it
And desecrate those gallstone eyes?

Unlucky opals, they looked and waited
As if my hand were a torch
To burn the bush around it
And smoke out its young.

Beads of blood broke over the leaves
When I disentangled my hand
And my boot lashed into empty space
Like a snake after its primeval prey—
Invisible as soon as it is seen.

Only a bloody hand was left.

I tell myself as if it's true
I wear an utterly complete disguise
Which is myself,
No one can recognise me through it
No one I know, and not myself
Who never would have thought
It could be so complete
As to deceive not only others
But most of all myself.

There are no eyes to penetrate
That utterly complete disguise
Except my own
Which cannot be blacked-out for long:
I begin to see through it
When no other person can
By knowing others better
Than I know myself—
Assailing their disguises
And thereby penetrating mine.

If it were possible to shift
This utterly complete disguise
I would despise myself
Through knowing nothing of what lies behind:
Know all the lies, betrayals and conceits
That foul up the clear water of the soul
In order to become one heart and wise,
And throw away that never utterly complete disguise.

He who continually travels
Will collapse on the road—
The one who stays at home
Will die in bed.

He who can love
Will die in pain;
The one who revels in intelligence
Will not wake up from sleep.

He who cannot act
Will sleep,
And he who does
Is killed by life.

I write at midnight
Eyes aching at the day's length
Blocking the porthole-elbow of Bothnia
One grand eye lit in midnight-yellow,
Turquoise and carmine sun—
A huge wound gouged by the night-dragon
No one can see.

Day won't bleed to death—
Flat sea flooding close enough to dip
My pen and write in.
No summer gun can shoot the sun
Give a final blast of mercy
And send it down to grapple with a death
Rising up soon for me.

Space and sun and midnight light
At last fill in my emptiness,
Till I sleep like the sun
And bleed into the cleansing sea so close,
That reddens like a Roman bath
While the black night-arrow is rotting in me.

Frontiers melt in salt-waste
Meet at burial mound or winter hut
Lake and forest stricken by frost-wind
Cross oilstain on danubes and caspians.
Wood outlives stone,

Asia or Europe, love shaped by stomach-ache
Heart-torn, internal bleeding of the brain
And pain the same wherever crashing:
Lovers whom dissimulating rivers rope or split
At any driving selfish will
Frontiers fragmented where sturgeon
Breed by reed and bargehull
In the caviar lands of Astrakhan.

Eurasian loveland wide as curving startracks over steppe and
    meadow:
Berdichev like a flower on the wingtip vanishes
And jetplane passengers eat their lunch
And crave the wilderness to taste its flint and thirst
And meet by chance or moonphase
The frontier that merges into frontier and into sleep.

Ice is breaking on the lake:
A bird's-head totem in the middle
Is staked to a reflected sunflame
That pierces the sinews of its feet.

Black ice smoulders all around. Dusk
Approaches without sound or reason.
Water below moves its shoulders
Like a giant craving to see snow.

Ninety degrees of bitterness preserve
Mosquito eggs. There is death
From fire but not by ice
As the fist of winter
Pulls into the mittens of the sun.

Summer warmth will mark these banks.
Fragmenting water has a single life:
Ice continues melting as I walk and look
At the domed sun touching the horizon:
The figure in the middle sinks
Till its feet touch bottom and reach fire.

Stopped his cart
Refused all food
Turned towards sun
Shook tin brass skulls copper
Pressed a horseshoe to his eyes
Evening on the shore of Lake Baikal:
Head between land and sky
Spun a waterspout of
Madness from a fountain heart
Hand five candle-fingers flaming
Grave-toes patterning the gravel
Rhyming tree all clothed in green
Chews the beansprouts of his crown
Million spondees bleeding in his teeth
Pipe dance pouring through his stomach-gutters,

Spins to music
Stick legs strut
Shouting shatters
Melt and planctify
Fisherboats and floating trees
Recites alone and long
One leg drawn into his skirt
Baikal fish and stork in one
Ignoring sea that threatens
Fire and spiders, copperbacks and claws
Creep from the rimline lake
Feet to feel and lips to taste
Have no heart but swarm
To eat from him and die of it—

As brasshooved breakers
Break and draw them back
And he blood-weaving
Over sand to green land
Melting and metalling in blacksmith power
Siberian tundra-giant singing
Horses birds and torches
Scorch all gutters of his stomach
Flesh of one man falling
Turn-spin-whirl-grin
Unfurl skinflags from his back and arms

Drop, and hear drums rend him
For the flight to heaven
And final plummeting at fire.

A famous writer dies just like the rest
No one deader than he is
As he lies in state
And people weep to consolidate their memories
Spread white flowers around his coffin
Stop his soul inside from eating the dissolving snow
But free of them he gets back to a thaw and green fields
At the end of summer,
New birds perching on his wet bare bones
Rainbows crossing ribcage and skull,
Then they fly south at the first subtle death-breath
Of crippled leaves and the leprosy of frost.

He could not do what they did
In their freedom
Make a body small enough
And with compliant feathers
And wings (and find the clean wet bones
Of a poor dead writer to rest on)
Take off to warm and living climates.

He got old and famous, lies
Honoured in a great hall
That people file through with white flowers
And dead eyes that melt
For a great dead author.
They walk slowly by to glance in guilt and sorrow
See his face and photograph
And give him all their human warmth
While his dead soul inside feeds on the dissolving snow.

Ride it, ride it out
Ride out this mare of sleeplessness
Galloping mad above the traffic hub
Of Gorki Street,
Weaving between Red stars
And the roar of cleaning-wagons.
(Today all Moscow was in mourning
Because there was no queue at Lenin's tomb.
I said: If you don't believe me go and see.
And now the familiar sight is there again!)

Ride out this beast who will not let me sleep
Who drags me up great Gorki Street and Pushkin Square
And Mayakovsky Square towards Leningrad glowing like a rose in
    the distant flat horizon of the northwest ringed by jewels of
    swamp and water and occasional faint smears of blood—
Pull up the blankets, and overpower with arms of sanity,
Be small for a few hours of the night.

We—I have destroyed you
WE—I have finished you off
Torn you out of me.

Those who live by WE
Can keep their smoking villages
And rows of graves,
Ancient frontiers
Or sentimental shores.

The wind had a good haul
Dragged that banner down
When atoms separated in the slime.
Scattering was fine and welcome—
No shout of WE as they ran for dry land.

WE—telephones can't speak or hear
Close their rubber gates
To the joined views of lovers that are not just
Unless saved for one another in the spite of wedlock.
Pity never lived in such false unities of WE.

Protective WE evoked instinctively
Doesn't stand in my defence,
Has no synonym or meaning
Except among like-minded people
Singing in their ecstasies of WE.

Not even two or three or country to join in—

Such things are not for me.
In the end not even you
Who may be writing this in any other lit-up darkness
Can bring a cry of WE
At this similarity and meeting
With its hint of recognition, and departure.

From the beginning
Poets have wanted
Everything to be the same.

Those who worship horseshoes
Or the moon are unified by
Wanting everything
To be the same.

Uniforms obsess them:
Trees of a certain sort
Match perfectly enough
To have one name.
Untold million flowers of one colour
Have one image in the catalogue.

Eyes are eyes—
Of different colours maybe,
Joined by a single look:
In the beginning was the word
And one book.

Everything must be the same
Before in basic truths
Poets can discover
Differences.

The poet sings his poems on a bridge
A bridge without shelter open to horizontal rain
And the steely nudge of lightning,
Or icy moths of snow that bring slow death
And smother him from sun and moon
Croon him to sleep by snow wings touching his eyes;

Through all this he sings,
No people coming close to watch when the snow
Melts and elemental water-forces smash
Between cliff and rock under his swaying bridge.
When the water thins, his sweat-drops burst
On the scorching rocks like sparks from a flower pod;
Through all this he sits and sings his poems
To those vague crowds on either bank
That he cannot consider or make out
With such short sight—for after the first applauded poem
He let his glasses smash onto the rocks below.

The bridge belongs to him, the only property he owns.
It grows no food, supports no houses
And so was cheap to purchase with the first mediocre poems.
It spans a river that divides two territories.
He knew it and made no mistake—
Today he faces one and tomorrow the other
But from blurred eyes they look the same to him:
Green fields and red roofed houses
Rising to mountains where wars can be fought
Without a bitter end being reached—
The same on either side. He does not write a poem every day
But each pet territory takes its turn
To hear his words in one set language burn
And drive them back from each other.

In any rash attack they cannot cross his bridge
But broach that river and ravine
Down at the estuary or right upstream.
He listens to the stunning bloodrush of their arms
And shakes his head, never grows older
As he bends it to his paper (which one side or the other
Still contrives to set, with food) by his hands' reach.
Sometimes sly messengers approach at night
Suggesting that he writes and then recites
Upon some momentary theme
To suit one side and damn the other,
At which he nods and smiles, tells jokes and riddles,
Agrees to everything and promises
That tomorrow he will tear the world apart
With his great reading.

He stays young, ignores all promises, requests and prophecies,
But his bridge grows old, the beams eaten and the ropes brittle
And some night alien figures in a half circle at each dim bridgehead
Brandish knives and axes. Lanterns flash,
Blades and points spark like spinning moons
Gathering nearer as he puts away his pens and parchment,
Closes his eyes to sleep, and does not wake up for a week
Knowing that some night he will once more dream
The familiar childhood dream
Of falling forever down the sheer side of the world—
And never wake up.

But he owns and dominates his bridge—
It is his bread and soul and only song:
If the people do not like it—they can cut him loose.

In order for certain people to survive it is necessary

To appear weak, yet bleed the world

To love, and wreck every family you can get your hands on, though never your own

To appear honest, upright and noble, yet know exactly when to twist the knife and do most damage

To be unable to say no, when asked a favour, yet do it so that who-ever asked it will live for years in anguish

To be unable to say yes to anything that benefits yourself, yet do it so that it benefits nobody else either;

To seem a friend when someone owes you money, and an enemy when you owe it to them;

Never to know where to settle down, nor where to set off for

To love every woman you see, but none in particular

To be true when truth is unimportant

To lie when it is vital

To be subtle when the sky is dark with migrating bird-clouds

To be plain and pompous when a friend does not know what to do with her life, and asks your advice because she is at the end of her tether and thinks you may be able to help her but won't because she might then go away and do it and so leave you alone to think about what you should do, which you never want to do because you might end up killing yourself which you are still not sure about;

To be silent when speech would ease a dozen hearts, and talk when it would break at least one;

To appear awkward when you denounce law and order, and con-fident when you extol chaos

To believe in Anarchy and Freedom yet curse when the bus is late

Love the working people and hate communism—except that one
day it might come to power and be the only thing that will
stop them getting at your throat
Like pop-music because it enables you to feel superior while at the
same time enjoying yourself
Be afraid of death and dying when the ejaculation of sperm into
the sweet womb is going to engulf you
Loathe life when the world goes dim at some unexplained and
universal catastrophic midnight that sends others running to
light fires or stuff bread into their mouths;
To smile at your dead mother, and weep bleak tears at the birth of
some child or other
To walk in rain and hide from the scalding water of the sun
Watch the sky when the tide is threatening your feet
Abandon all you love and run towards what you hate if it means
leaving safety and comfort, and at the same time retreat from
those far-off mountains caught in the eternal heat-fire of freedom and vengeance—
To have your name struck from you
So that you treasure your passport which robs you of identity because it exists, and stops you asking: Who am I? in order to
know one day what you are;
Appear to confess everything, so as to tell nothing, and ardently
explain so as to properly mystify:
To ask advice from everyone, but allow no one to tell you what to
do,
To search after death and chaos with fanatic diligence and calm,
yet survive as an example of goodness and virtue to the world.

LOVE IN THE ENVIRONS OF VORONEZH

Love in the environs of Voronezh
It's far away, a handsome town
But what has it to do with love?
Guns and bombers smashed it down.

Yet love rebuilt it street by street
The dead would hardly know it now
And those who live forget retreat.

There's no returning to the heart:
The dead to the environs go
Away from resurrected stone.

Reducible to soil and snow
They hem the town in hard as bone:
Beyond the outer zones of Voronezh.